Oh, The Things You Can Do

A Kid's Guide to Happiness

Written by
Kara Lea Fleming

Illustrated by
Anchal Gupta

iUniverse books may be ordered through booksellers or by contacting:

iUniverse
1663 Liberty Drive
Bloomington, IN 47403
www.iuniverse.com
844-349-9409

Because of the dynamic nature of the Internet, any web addresses or links contained
in this book may have changed since publication and may no longer be valid. The views
expressed in this work are solely those of the author and do not necessarily reflect the
views of the publisher, and the publisher hereby disclaims any responsibility for them.

Any people depicted in stock imagery provided by Getty Images are models,
and such images are being used for illustrative purposes only.
Certain stock imagery © Getty Images.

ISBN: 978-1-6632-1179-8 (sc)
ISBN: 978-1-6632-1178-1 (hc)
ISBN: 978-1-6632-1180-4 (e)

Library of Congress Control Number: 2020920855

Print information available on the last page.

iUniverse rev. date: 11/18/2020

This book is dedicated to my sons, Ben and Finn. You are both my pride and joy and I couldn't be more proud to be your Mommy. Always know, however far apart we may be, we will always be together. I love you.

We all have big feelings,
some good and some bad.
What fills up your heart?
What makes you feel glad?

So many things that we face every day
can cause either pain or memories that stay.

Think

Feel

Do

You are never alone: we're connected; it's true.
It's about ...
what you think, how you feel, what you do.

When life gets you down, it's important to see
what you need to do to make you happy.
There's no magic pill that will help you restart.
You need to do things that fill up your heart.

Positive thoughts may take practice for you
but will help you feel better; just start with a few.
Wake in the morning, smile, and say,
"If I think happy thoughts, I will have a good day."

We all make mistakes and can have a bad day.
When we're unkind to others, it's important to say,

"I'm sorry I hurt you. Please forgive me."
You'll feel better after giving an apology.

Always choose kindness; don't follow the crowd.
Making good choices will help you feel proud.

When your feelings are hurt, do you let someone know?
It's important so anger does not start to grow.

Talk to a parent, a teacher, or a friend,
whoever can help your broken heart mend.

That person can help you with what you should do
to get back on track when you're feeling blue.

Sad and mad feelings can change if you cope.
Do something to change them; don't give up hope.

Whatever can ease your tense body and mind,
help you feel better and slowly unwind.

Scream in a pillow; try punching it hard,
or find a quiet place in your backyard.

Your needs are important; you need to feel good.
So make sure you do things that you know you should.

Is it a walk or a run with a friend?
Or reading a book from beginning to end?

You might need to draw, play piano, bike ride,
play guitar, kick a ball, get fresh air outside.

Write in a journal.

Bake cookies with Mom.

Go fishing with Dad.

Do Yoga to stay calm.

Play a game with your brother.

Talk to a friend.

Make up a new dance.

Help someone on the mend.

Plant flowers outside.

Clean up your room.

Find a new hobby.

Help with chores. Grab a broom!

Listen to music, and sing it out loud.
Think of something you did that made you feel proud.
Ask for help if you need it; you'll need to at times.
Support from your loved ones will help ease your mind.

We are all so different in what we must do
to help keep us strong when we feel blue.

Be strong. Find yourself. You don't need permission.
Be the best version of you. Make it your mission.

Make a list of the things that make you feel great.
Do the things you write down. It is never too late.

My List:

_____

_____

_____

_____

_____

_____

_____

_____

Printed in the United States
By Bookmasters